D0733003

PARENTING

WITH *Sanity* & *Joy*

PARENTING

WITH &

101 SIMPLE STRATEGIES

SUSAN G. GRONER

ILLUSTRATIONS BY SANNA MANDER

Paperback ISBN: 978-1-951412-04-3
Ebook ISBN: 978-1-951412-14-2
LCCN: 2019915952

Manufactured in China.

Design by Andrea Kelly

10 9 8 7 6 5 4 3 2 1

The Collective Book Studio
Oakland, California
www.thecollectivebook.studio

To my parents, and to all the parents
that I have learned from and continue to learn from.
I use your lessons every day.

—Sue

Your children are not your children.
They are the sons and daughters of Life's
longing for itself.

—*Kahlil Gibran*

In This Book...

Opening Words	8
Parenting Golden Rules	11
Family Time	27
Rules and Respect	47
Perspective and Judgment	65
Gratitude and Attitude	91
Food and Dining	107
Forbidden Phrases	123
Life Skills	137
Family Management	161
About the Author	173
Acknowledgements	176

Opening Words

When I was a young mother, I was constantly second-guessing my parenting decisions. How much screen time? How much allowance? What type of chores? Music lessons or sports? Scheduled time or downtime? The list was endless.

Friends, articles, and parenting books provided plenty of advice. I would read a chapter or two (who has time to read a whole book?) and embark on a new parenting direction. My husband could always tell when I had embraced a "New Plan" because I would start enforcing new regulations and change how I spoke to the kids. Worst of all, I would become anxious anew that I had been doing everything all wrong. How would my children ever become the smartest, nicest, and most talented kids in the world given that I had messed things up so badly?

What I have come to realize since is that every child, every parent, and every family unit functions differently, and there is no one answer or directive that will work for everyone. Still, most of us want the same thing—for our children to be safe, for our children to feel loved, and for our children to grow up to be confident, capable, caring adults. On top of that, I wanted to feel good while raising my children. My goal was to find parenting strategies that did not suck the joy out of being a parent.

I have tried many approaches, some with better results than others. One revelation for me was when I decided to let myself become visibly excited about giving my children permission to do something they really wanted to do, rather than behave as if I were reluctantly doing them a big favor. This little shift in attitude helped to make a big difference in my relationship with my kids.

I was first encouraged to write this book by Dayna Steele, who thought I could offer parents some practical, actionable skills to help them improve their parenting. The tips I have culled here are meant to help you relax and find more enjoyment on the route to raising resilient, self-sufficient young adults. This book is designed to be an easy-to-read, pick-up-every-now-and-then reference that may help you look at your parenting style in a different light. If you find a tip that resonates with you, give it a try. If it does not work for you, let it go. Most important, do not get down on yourself if you have been doing things differently. The mere fact that you are reading this book makes you a good parent. It means you are making an effort and that you care.

I hope what I have put together here helps other parents feel more confident, competent, and inspired in discovering what works best for their families.

I think we are defined by
the way we treat ourselves and
the way we treat other people.

—*Oprah Winfrey*

CHAPTER 1

PARENTING GOLDEN RULES

Say YES with joy

If you know you are ultimately going to drive your child to the mall, let your daughter have a 3-person sleepover or allow your son an extra cookie after dinner—just go straight to a happy YES! When you offer up an awesome gesture as if you are doing your kids a big favor, it takes the fun out of it. It is so easy to add joy to your delivery with "Sure!" or "I'd be happy to!" or "Let's do that!" Your enthusiasm will make your child feel even better about your YES, but best of all, it will make you feel great.

Do not brag about your child

When someone brags about how exceptional their child is, do you ever feel, a teeny-tiny bit, as if your child does not measure up? Well, that is how other parents feel when you brag about your child. As parents, we need to keep this tendency in check. Your child may be exceptional, but leave the heralding for the grandparents.

3

Respect your team

Teachers, coaches, lesson instructors—they are all a part of your parenting team. Your child may be benched or not performing well at school, and you may be frustrated, but do not yell at or blame someone else. Your child needs to see you treat the authority figures in their lives with respect. Do ask privately and politely if there is something your child could do to thrive more in that environment. Lots can get accomplished through teamwork. Little gets done through finger-pointing or blaming.

Do not discipline other children

This can get ugly, really fast. Every parent has his or her own way of disciplining, and most are not comfortable with (or appreciative of) someone else taking on that role. Unless the child is in real danger, leave it alone. If a child is being rude in your home or not abiding by your rules, you can simply ask for the child to leave. (Call the parent and explain delicately.) You may even want to explain to the child that he or she is welcome back when they are comfortable following the rules of your home. Anything beyond that is just not your place.

Pay attention to timing, manner, and intonation (TMI)

You know what is likely to set your children off. Do not bring up something stressful the night before an exam or when they are tired or hungry. Talk about "tough topics" with an "easy" attitude. Keep your word choices neutral and scrub your vocal inflections clean of any hint of judgment, blame, or negativity. Timing, manner, and intonation can make all the difference in how easily (and willingly) your child is able to engage with you.

6

Leave your past in the past

When you tell your children, "You don't know how lucky you are . . . ," you are inadvertently burdening them with your old baggage. When a child hears about your past struggles, they take some of that inside themselves. They cannot do anything about your past and they should not feel as though they must. Stories about your own tough fourth-grade teacher are okay as long as they are stories you would share at a dinner party. Anything touchier than that, leave for your own BFFs.

Turn off your phone

When you are with your child, set your phone to Do Not Disturb. Or better yet, put it away. This gesture says, "Right now, there is nothing more important than you!" Setting aside time when you can unplug and not be interrupted is essential to quality time with your children. They will know you are with them 100 percent. And as a bonus, you are setting a great example by not being glued to your phone.

Spend time with people you like

Stop hanging out with people that don't make you feel good about yourself or your parenting. You are not obligated to be friends with or spend time with anyone, even if they are parents of your children's friends. Showing your kids that there is no place in your life for people who bring you down will help your kids learn to navigate their own friendships.

It's okay to do something for yourself

Whether it's getting a babysitter for an hour or hiring a housekeeper occasionally, we all need assistance sometimes to find some essential alone time. Accept offers of help from friends or family and don't be afraid to ask for what you need. Nap during your child's nap time. Watch mindless television. Take a bath. Call a friend. These short, relaxing snippets of time are not only extremely valuable to your health and well-being, they will help you be a more relaxed parent.

One thing I had learned from
watching chimpanzees with their infants
is that having a child should be fun.

—*Jane Goodall*

CHAPTER 2

FAMILY TIME

Our Family Traditions:

10

Create your own family traditions

You can build "We always . . ." moments around practically anything. "We always wake up to a treasure hunt on our birthdays." "We always play I Spy on long car rides." "We always celebrate the last day of school with ice cream in the park." Even if your kids get old enough that they groan when you start performing the Snow Day Dance, deep down they like it. Innocent traditions like these help weave the fabric of family legacy.

Celebrate family milestones together

Moving into a big kid bed. Learning to ride a bike. Losing a tooth. Getting braces off. You can avoid having one child feel left out of another child's accomplishment by making it a point to celebrate everyone's milestones as a family. This is an opportunity for siblings to learn to be supportive of one another and enjoy each other's big moments and successes.

12

Share your fun childhood stories

Tell your kids about fun facts or happenings from when you were a child, especially stories that correspond to your child's current age. Were you mischievous? Did you forget lines in the school play? Were you a class clown? Did you and your friends have a secret fort in the woods? Kids love to hear these stories, and they'll probably ask you to tell them over and over. These anecdotes make you more relatable and sometimes open the door to kids sharing more about their own world. Just remember to leave your negative stories behind.

Activities We'd Like to do Together:

13

Try something new as a family

Is there an activity you have been wanting to try? Cooking a new recipe with some first-time ingredients. Exploring a new town. Maybe you have never been hiking. Now is the time. Have family members take turns at coming up with the ideas. You're sure to have a lot of fun, and you'll create great memories. You might even invent new family traditions.

Start meals with a family question

"How was your day?" is a legitimate thing to ask, but it rarely leads to real conversation and more often shuts it down. Instead, make mealtime sharing fun by creating a set of family questions that keep the conversation flowing. Get help from games like Table Topics, or even better, let the kids take turns helping to write them—they may have things they want to ask you about, too. Encourage new questions and add them to your list. Keep the list handy at meal time to help start real conversations.

Spend alone time with each child

There is no substitute for one-on-one time with each child. Positive, focused attention helps to build and maintain an emotional connection. If you can swing 10 to 15 minutes every day, great. If you can't, make sure your kids know spending alone time with them is important to you and schedule it whenever possible. To make the most of this time, do whatever your child wants. That might be building a tower or playing make-believe. If your kids are older, maybe ask them to teach you how to play their favorite video game or show you a favorite app.

Play board games together

Board games are not just fun, they offer opportunities to shake up family roles. Games like
Chutes and Ladders require luck, not skill, so the
littlest family members can win fair and square.
Some kids will rule in games like Pictionary, Apples to Apples, and Taboo where being able to
anticipate how another player thinks gives you
a big advantage. In other words, different board
games allow different people's strengths to be
rewarded. So, mix up the repertoire and may the
best player win.

Who to Call:

17

Schedule a regular call with family members

Weekly calls with your parents and your in-laws is a good place to start. This is not only a great way for your children and their grandparents (aunts, uncles, etc.) to build and maintain close relationships, but it also provides tons of pleasure for Grandma and Grandpa. Nothing beats real visits, but video calls are second best.

18

Laugh with your kids

There is plenty of science behind the fact that laughing increases bonding hormones and decreases stress hormones. Laughing will not only strengthen your relationships with your children, it may also help them to sleep better and to be more cooperative. And of course, laughing with your spouse can lead to other great things . . .

Offline Family Activities We Enjoy:

19

Unplug as a family

Spend time together as a family completely un-plugged and doing activities offline. Try a fam-ily bike ride, hike, or play hide-and-seek. Have a sing-along, juggle, build a snowman. Make a batch of popcorn, snuggle up together, and read. Turning off phones (and other devices) and stow-ing them out of sight allows time for focused family fun, relaxation, and interaction. If you can do this regularly, it will become a welcome and enjoyable respite for everyone. Perhaps for you most of all!

Loving a child doesn't mean giving in to all his whims;
to love him is to bring out the best in him,
to teach him to love what is difficult.

—*Nadia Boulanger*

CHAPTER 3

RULES AND RESPECT

20

Say NO with conviction

NO should not be your go-to, knee-jerk response. But when you do say NO, make sure you mean it. If you are not sure, give yourself time to think with a "Let me get back to you on that." Once you deliver your NO, stick to your guns and do not leave the door open for your child's attempts to negotiate. Nicely say, "I have made my decision" and walk away or resume whatever you were doing. There is no need to feel guilty about saying NO. You know what is best for your child. NO does not mean you are being mean. It means you are being a conscientious parent.

Set boundaries

Family boundaries are personal and individual and arise from asking yourself what you consider non-negotiable. For example, "In this family, we never treat each other with disrespect" is an expectation that stems from your values and a position from which you will not budge. When your child knows that sitting in the front seat of the car before she is old enough is never, ever, ever going to happen, she will come to understand that asking is futile. Knowing where you draw the line helps your child feel safe.

Stoop to their level—literally

When having an important conversation, try to be eye to eye with your children instead of talking to them from above (literally, "talking down to them"). What you say will be heard more openly; they will feel less intimidated. Sit together on the floor and hold your child on your lap, or if you are standing, maybe let your child sit on a counter. If your child is already taller than you, have your discussions sitting down.

23

Set rules

Rules are simply stated guidelines and expectations. They usually refer to behaviors that, when followed, make life run more smoothly. The main reason to have rules is so you do not have to revisit every situation every time it comes up. If your rule is no phones at mealtime, then there is no need to discuss it each time you sit down to eat. Rules are not optional and should be consistently enforced. Unlike boundaries, there are times when rules can be broken, or even reviewed and updated. However, each time you "bend" a rule, you run the risk of diminishing how your children view what is expected of them, so proceed with caution.

24

Let kids help make the rules

When they are old enough, it is great to have kids participate in the rule-making. When your children are invested in the rules, they will better understand their usefulness and will be more inclined to follow them. Their participation will also help them feel more respected as family members. Allow children to revisit and reevaluate the rules with you as needed. Win, win, win!

Set limits

Limits are typically for things that can be quantified: bedtime, the number of cookies allowed after dinner, how much time to spend in front of a screen, the number of consecutive days a bath can be skipped, etc. You can even set limits on how many times your child can whine on Saturdays. Life is not a free-for-all, and limits help us manage that slippery place between what we want and what is good for us. Setting limits for your children teaches them how to set limits for themselves.

Use an imaginary leash

Have you ever seen one of those extension leashes for dogs? The dog is tethered, but the leash extends (by a lot) to give the dog room to explore. Use this image to offer some independence and freedom to your child. Each year, allow the leash to get a little longer. Maybe they can walk farther with friends, or they can make their own decisions about how to spend their birthday money. You can always give the leash a gentle tug if need be. By senior year of high school, your child should be able to function with almost complete independence; the leash should be gone!

27

Respect your child's privacy

Keeping your child safe may sometimes require you to be in their business, but as much as possible, try to run a home where everyone respects each other's physical privacy. When people share a living space, it's important for everyone in the family to feel they have some privacy. Make it a norm for your children to knock on your bedroom door before walking in and for everyone to have privacy in the bathroom. Of course, there are times you will want your kids to keep their bedroom doors open, but it is always nice and respectful to knock.

28

Speak softly

When you really want your kids to listen, keep your message to a few words and deliver it more quietly than your normal speaking voice. The quieter the voice the bigger the impact.

Be consistent

Here is the reason children thrive on consistency: When life is predictable, it makes them feel safe. The best way to end up with dependable kids is for you to model consistency—with rules, with your expectations of them and their responsibilities, and most important, in how you handle your own responsibilities.

30

Do nothing

Sometimes it is best to let situations play out on their own. That means: do not interfere, do not get involved, do not engage. If your children are arguing, let them. If they come to you to complain, respond with a simple, "Oh." Your kids will learn to sort things out on their own, because they know you are not going to get involved or take sides. Bonus: this will create less sibling rivalry.

31

Be a receptive and active listener

When your son is having a bad day, just listen. You don't have to jump in with a solution or life lesson, or deliver a speech. All you need to do is be with him the way you would hope your best friend would be with you—with open ears and an open heart. Make it your mission to discover what your child is trying to tell you. Listening is a skill you will get better at the more you do it. Look for facial expressions that may not match what he is actually saying. Then, repeat back in your own words what you think you heard. This kind of validation lets your child know you are really listening and you think his issues are important. You are also helping your child build better communication skills by modeling yours.

Suggested questions to ask:

What do you think about what's going on?

What do you think you could do?

What could you do differently next time?

What do you wish you had said?

How might you resolve this?

How did what [that person] said or did, make you feel?

Ask kids what they think

Rather than just launching into your own opinions about a problem your child is having with a friend or about a situation at school or even about something going on in your lives together, use probing questions to find out where your child stands on the issue. Remember the active listening tip! Everyone likes to know their opinion is valued and needed.

One of the most frustrating aspects of parenting is that there is no school for it. You learn by doing.

—*Dr. Elliot Barsh, Pediatrician*

CHAPTER 4

PERSPECTIVE AND JUDGMENT

33

Don't cry (or yell) over spilled milk

Accidents happen. If your son knocks over a glass of milk while you're frantically trying to get dinner on the table, it may seem like a big deal, but it's not. Keep things light—"Oh, don't you hate when that happens?"—and throw him a towel, so he can wipe it up. Children falter, as do adults. They get paint on their favorite pants. They lose their most cherished toy—again. Don't harp on every little mishap. Your child already feels bad enough about those things. Practice cutting your child a break. Not only will this create a happier home, but your accepting attitude will teach your kids to cut themselves (and others) a break when the millions of silly little things that go wrong in life inevitably pop up.

34

Do not compare

Some children are organized. Some children love to read. Some children like having lots of friends. Some children eat anything you put in front of them. Every child has strengths. And, every child has weaknesses. Comparing your child to another, whether it is their friend, their brother, or the son of your high school bestie, does not make them feel good. If you believe your child is falling short in bedroom tidiness, approach the topic directly—talk about their toys on the floor and their unmade bed—rather than making them feel like they are not as good as someone else.

Embrace boredom

If your daughter is bored, it does not mean you need to drop whatever you're doing to entertain her. This is a short-term solution that serves only to let your child know that boredom needs to be fixed, and you are the one who will fix it. Explain that not every moment of every day is scintillating. Remind her that she has the best tool to make anything more interesting: her own imagination. When you help your children learn how to find or make their own fun, they get to have a life where routine or tedious experiences (like doing laundry or waiting in line) are not things to dread, and can even be brain-freeing moments to look forward to.

Don't worry about their college until high school

Your child will probably get into college even if she has not become the best violin player in your time zone by second grade. You will meet parents that try to convince you otherwise, but only because someone already convinced them. Childhood and adolescence are times to try different things and discover what you like. Most kids who are groomed for college through some activity end up hating it by the time they apply. College is just another period in your child's life; it's not the end game. If college doesn't fit into your child's plans, support the decision to attend a trade school, acquire a specialized certification, or pursue anything else she might need to follow her dreams and passions.

Have realistic expectations

If you expect things to be perfect, you will un-
doubtedly be disappointed—often. If you expect
that things will sometimes go wrong, you can relax and laugh about it when they do. Planning
your child's birthday party? Arranging a special
evening with your partner? Looking forward to
a family afternoon? Enjoy the planning and the
process, but don't expect a flawless event. Ad-
justing expectations helps you go with the flow.

38

Your child is not a Mini-Me

This may come as a shocker, but your child is going to like things you don't like and may be interested in things you're not interested in. Just because you loved playing piano, doesn't mean they will. They may love dancing even if you have two left feet. Rather than directing your child toward your interests and talents and thereby discounting their own dreams and passions, offer them opportunities to discover what they love. Don't worry. There will be plenty of other ways your little apple falls close to the tree.

Lose the P word

Move away from "Perfect" in all its forms: perfectly . . . perfected . . . perfection. Striving for perfection can create unnecessary stress for you and your children. It also causes disappointment as it's usually an unobtainable goal. Kids often avoid trying something new because they don't think they will be successful. So instead of evaluating the result, praise for hard work and effort. Similarly, you do not have to be a Super Mom to be a great mom. Rather than judging yourself against a perfect ideal, praise yourself for what you have done and start to embrace the delicious feeling of being "good enough."

40

Failure is your friend

Every chance you get, let your child know failure is merely one step in the learning process. Let him know frustration is not only normal but a necessary part of mastering something new. Let him see you struggle to learn something. Likely, your child sees you doing only what you are already good at. Share with him out loud what you think you might do differently next time you attempt that pineapple upside-down cake. And, ask him what he might do differently if he is having trouble landing that kick flip. There is no such thing as failure if you learn something from it moving forward.

Call your childhood self to mind

Try to remember what you were like as a child or teen. Be honest. Were you the super-organized person you are today? Did you do everything you were told? Were you the perfect specimen of a child and after you they broke the mold? Chances are, the answer to each of these questions is no. It takes a long time for the rational, good-sense, non-impulsive part of our brains to develop fully; estimates are 25 years! Children are evolving into the grown-ups they will eventually become—just as you did. Keep that in mind.

Everyone is different

This seems obvious, but it's worth reminding yourself you and your child are not necessarily wired the same way. She may not be organized by nature. He may not be a morning person. You may be a procrastinator and have a child who gets stressed out when she is not on time. We all march to the beat of our own drum, and when you parent to their beat, rather than the beat you think they should be playing, you and your child can develop a lovely rhythm together.

43

Do not pick or judge your children's friends

At some point, your child will have a friend or two (or three) who you just don't care for. A tough guy, a queen bee, a kid with no manners, a youngster who is not as studious as you would like. Resist the urge to "shield" your child and keep your negative opinions to yourself. A friend that does not fit your child's usual mold may fill a need you are not aware of. Maybe your daughter needs a break from feeling like such an academic, and she wants to try and fit in more with the cool kids. Maybe this friendship is an opportunity for her to learn how to put on a little makeup or master a video game. Let your children learn to feel confident maneuvering the ups and downs of friends and cliques on their own.

44

Pick your battles

Not everything is worth an argument. If your son wants to hang posters in his room, but you don't think they go with the décor, or you don't want to ruin the walls, or you simply don't like them, first ask yourself: Is my child going to get hurt by doing this? Is anyone going to get hurt? Is this really a big deal in the grand scheme of things? This brief line of questioning can be employed for clothing choices, food choices, movie choices— practically anything. Your ability to not sweat the small stuff will not only keep the peace, it also helps your child understand the importance of things you do need to clamp down on.

45

Adjust your attitude about mistakes

Telling your children to learn from their mistakes is a great lesson—one of the most important—but you need to walk the walk. Shifting your own idea about mistakes or problems changes your worldview. What if you taught your children to welcome their mistakes and talk about them, rather than live life trying to avoid them? What if you sat down at dinner and said, "What mistakes did we each make today?" What if everyone in your family felt they could share mishaps without feeling judged? You can almost hear the sighs of relief.

46

Do not dismiss your children's concerns

Kids' concerns can seem random and outlandish; your job is to figure out what they are really asking. "Mommy, what if you get really sick?" probably means "Who is going to take care of me?" Telling your daughter that her concern is ridiculous and you are never going to be that sick will not make her feel safe. Children feel anxious about a lot of things they don't yet know how to put into words. Concrete information can quell that anxiety. "If I ever get really sick, Aunt Tilly will come to stay." Children always feel better if they know you have things under control or have a plan.

Ignore the judgy parents

Parent opinions vary widely on how to raise children: how kids should dress, which movies they should be able to watch, how much screen time they should be allowed, what they should eat, how they are disciplined in public. The list is endless and exhausting. One day, you will get "the look" from another parent or a group of parents. Remind yourself that your job is not to raise your child based on someone else's opinions or methods. Be clear about your own values and ignore the rest.

You Might Not Want to Say:

I would never let my kid . . .

How could you allow your child to . . .

You shouldn't . . .

My kids never/always . . .

I can't believe they let their kids . . .

48

Don't you be judgy either

If you might accidentally be that parent, try and remember that most parents are doing the very best they can. If you believe you have helpful, non-judgmental advice that can be delivered in a non-offensive way—in other words, kindly and with understanding—try it once and see how it goes. If the parent bristles or seems put off, feel free to step away from your Perfect Parent Mission and join the rest of us down here in the trenches.

Instead of: You are such an amazing Lego builder!

Try: You must feel very proud of what you've built.

Instead of: You are sooo beautiful!

Try: Your smile gives off so much love.

Instead of: You are the most talented dancer!

Try: It seems like you are really enjoying dancing.

Instead of: Good job!

Try: It looks like you are having so much fun! I can see how hard you were concentrating.

Monitor praise

Children need an internal voice that lets them know how capable they are. The way they develop that is not by being told repeatedly and excessively they are the best thing that has ever happened to humanity. Use your children's accomplishments to engage them in developing their own internal voices. As much as possible, avoid phrases like "You are the BEST . . . ," You are incredible," or "You are sooo talented!" You want to help build your child's self-esteem from the inside out, not the outside in.

What separates privilege from entitlement is gratitude.

—*Brené Brown*

CHAPTER 5

GRATITUDE AND ATTITUDE

Before you buy,
ask yourself:

- Does my child need this?

- Did my child do something special to earn this?

- Is this a special item better saved to give at a major holiday?

- Is this an item that my child should save up for and buy themselves?

Don't overindulge

Overdoing it with toys, clothes, and gifts creates long-term problems. It sets an expectation in our children that they should be showered with "stuff" all the time. In addition to fostering a mindset of instant gratification, it creates children who grow up with a sense of entitlement. Ask yourself why you feel the need to give, give, give. When a child has time to dream about something she wants and must also learn to wait for that thing, it sets the groundwork for lifelong motivation and coping skills. Provide for your children based on your vision of the adults you hope they become.

Practice empathy

Sympathy is when you feel sorry for someone; it usually leaves the person feeling like a victim. Empathy is when you let someone know you understand, and it leaves them feeling less alone with their troubles. Your 5-year-old son is upset because he got a chocolate cupcake rather than a vanilla cupcake at a birthday party. You do not have to fix things; you simply need to validate them. "Oh sweetie, I can see you are really disappointed. I would feel sad too if I didn't get my favorite flavor." Try empathy when your fifth grade daughter does not get the teacher she wants, or your teen cannot wear his favorite jeans, because they are in the laundry. Empathy is an emotion diffuser and a relationship builder.

52

Talk about gift-getting

If half your life is spent on picking up, sorting, and storing toys, your child may have enough of them. Before your son's birthday party invitations go out, assess with him whether he would like to do gifts differently this time. Some gifts can be donated to a homeless shelter. Or he can tell party guests he's raising money for a local charity and ask them to bring a donation ($7 for a 7-year-old!). Do not force your children to forego the gifts, but offer them the opportunity to experience how giving can be 100 times more satisfying than receiving.

Our Family Would Like to Help:

53

Engage in family service projects

Doing service as a family creates connection and closeness. It feels good to help other people, and it feels good to grow up in a family that does it together. Aside from instilling social consciousness and providing for those in need, service work opens your child's heart in a way few other things can. Find a local community organization to support. Engage children in the discovery. You can serve meals at a shelter or descend on an elderly neighbor's weedy lawn. There is no shortage of ways to help. And, there are no limits to the benefits of offering service.

54

Schedule family donation time

Set aside a few times throughout the year, perhaps at the end of each season, to gather old clothes, linens, toys, and any other items you want to discard, and donate the gently-used items to a local charity. Each family member should find at least a few items of their own to contribute. This is a good way to clean out closets, drawers, toy chests, garages, cabinets, everything! Clothes that are no longer worn, toys no longer played with, items with missing lids—get rid of them. Sometimes you even find things you were looking for or things you forgot you had.

How we help at home:

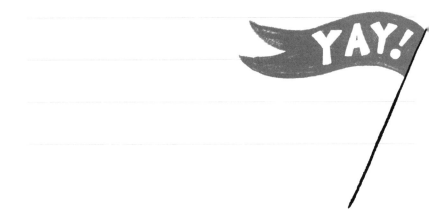

Replace chores with contributions

One easy way to make chores not seem like such a chore is to stop calling them that. Instead, they become family contributions. Teach your 2-year-old to collect dirty clothes into a basket. Have your 7-year-old water the plants. Explain to the kids that you are all on the same team working for household success. Be a cheerleader rather than a drill sergeant. When kids are pitching in— no matter what size the contribution—life skills are learned, families grow closer, and it is another inoculation against the entitlement epidemic.

56

Smile big and often

Smiling is not only a result of happiness, some research suggests it may also be the cause. When you smile, you're apt to be less stressed, less bothered by what is going on around you, and probably more likely to be heard by your child. Your tone changes when you are smiling; your child can hear the difference, and it sets the tone for the energy in your home. Smiling is easy, free, and infectious. Go ahead. Make your day!

57

Teach and model gratitude

Studies show people who feel gratitude are less depressed, better able to handle stress, and more optimistic. Tell your children what you feel grateful for. Regularly. Don't just leave this for Thanksgiving. Some days it may just be gratitude for whoever invented mint toothpaste or chocolate. An attitude of gratitude lets your child go through life looking for what is awesome. How awesome is that?

58

Practice random acts of kindness together

Look for opportunities to perform random acts of kindness in front of your kids and encourage them to do the same. Help someone cross the street, hold open a door, say something nice to a stranger. Without making it too big a deal, talk about what it felt like to do something nice and unexpected. Talk about what they imagine the other person felt like. And, if someone holds a door open for you, take a moment to mention how it made you feel. "I love when that happens!" sends a loud and clear message to kids how easy it is to be kind and how much it is appreciated.

The most remarkable thing about my mother
is that for thirty years she served the family
nothing but leftovers. The original meal
has never been found.

—*Calvin Trillin*

CHAPTER 6

FOOD AND DINING

59

Branch out from the kids menu

Use restaurant meals to help your child develop a taste for new foods. If your son insists on the mac and cheese from the kids menu, make a rule that he needs to taste something from the grown-up menu, too. If your daughter doesn't care for something, ask her why. It might be the texture, or the sauce, or something entirely different. Let kids know there are lots of options beyond chicken fingers.

Let kids order their own meals

Telling a waitperson what he would like to have for dinner allows your child to practice many skills: speaking to grown-ups they don't know, using "please" and "thank you," advocating on their own behalf, maintaining eye contact, asking questions if they are unsure about something. Restaurants are a safe, low-pressure environment where you can easily come to the rescue in a face-saving manner if things go awry.

Keep cookies around

Kids like to be places where there are good snacks. Having something fun to nibble on is a way of making your kids' friends feel welcome. If you are a family that does not typically do cookies or junk food, keep a guest stash of snacking options that won't make eyes roll. Not everyone wants to nibble on quinoa squares. Crazy, but true.

62

Have kids prepare their own meals

Spreading peanut butter on bread, pouring a bowl of cereal, or rinsing off an apple are good for starters and make your kids feel capable. Having a repertoire that includes more than ripping open a bag of chips gives them more freedom and independence (and healthy choices) around after-school snacks. It's never too early for a child to start learning his way around food. Plus, the more competent your child is in the kitchen, the more appetizing breakfast in bed will be on your birthday!

Avoid turning food into a control issue

If your child refuses to eat a meal, you do not need to make them eat. They will eat at the next meal. Skipping a meal is no big deal. If your daughter is hungry, let her make a peanut butter and jelly sandwich for herself. For young children, this is one of the few areas where they have control and they will begin to learn that they have the ability to prepare simple meals or snacks for themselves. Power struggles around food and eating are something you want to avoid. Try and keep meals about connecting as a family; do not make food and mealtime a war zone.

Be a role model with your own eating habits

If you do not want your kids to eat standing at the counter or picking the crumbs off the coffee cake, do not let them see you do it. Ditto if you do not want them to eat the exact same thing for every single meal. Overeating, undereating, picky eating, speed eating—they are going to learn a lot from you. What sort of food role model are you?

Some Dinner Topics:

What are you grateful for today?

What would you like to do this weekend?

Who do you admire and why?

Where in the world would you like to go?

Tell me a funny story.

What made you smile today?

What is your favorite family memory?

If you could have anything in the world, what would it be?

What are you most afraid of?

Have family dinner often

Family dinners are linked to everything from higher self-esteem to lower incidences of substance abuse. If you or your partner work too late to make this realistic, maybe try a family milk and cookies before bedtime. Or a family breakfast a few times a week. Coming together regularly, all of you, sets family time as an important commitment. Even if it seems inconvenient, kids grow to value this stabilizing ritual in their lives.

66

Have kids participate
in meal prep and clean-up

Peeling carrots. Setting the table. Pouring water. Clearing dishes. Filling the dishwasher. There is practically no end to what your child can help you with. It doesn't need to be a big something, but it should be a regular something. Teach your child early that meals don't just happen and many hands make light work. Helping allows kids of all ages to feel useful and important. It also teaches kids that being helpful is awesome.

67

Use the 80/20 rule

Do not create a life of stress around food. Eighty percent of the time, try to eat healthy foods, organic when you can, avoiding excessive sugar and carbs. The other twenty percent of the time, relax and enjoy. The stress of trying to eat only organic, grass-fed, whole-grain, unprocessed, extra-virgin everything can be worse for your health than occasionally eating food that's not ideal. This rule of thumb will also help older children navigate the junk food wasteland when you are not around.

68

Sometimes break the rules

Breaking food rules not only makes you seem more fun, it also helps kids understand diets that are too restrictive are not what life is about. Offer ice cream for breakfast or pancakes for dinner. Let them pick whatever unconventional meal they want on their birthday or packed for their school lunch. Have a no-veggie vacation! Breaking food rules occasionally is silly and fun, and nobody will get hurt. Your children will think this is the greatest thing ever.

Speak a word of affirmation at the
right moment in a child's life, and it's like lighting
up a whole roomful of possibilities.

—*Gary Smalley*

CHAPTER 7

FORBIDDEN PHRASES

What did you do in school today?

After a full day of school and other activities, your children may want to chill by themselves to unwind, download, or regroup. Most kids need to decompress when they get home. Leave them alone and don't start asking about their day until dinnertime. Instead, tell them about your day. If they're getting in the car, play some music they like. When they come off the school bus, have a snack waiting. These little acts show love.

Leave me alone

When your child wants to spend time with you, hearing you say, "leave me alone" can feel hurtful. Even adults don't want to hear this from anyone. If your daughter wants your attention, but you need to be alone, explain this to her; tell her when you will be available and how you look forward to spending time with her. If she doesn't yet tell time, keep a little kitchen timer on hand, set it, and ask her to come get you when it goes off. If you need to be alone because you are exhausted and need some me-time, explain this, too. They may be kids, but they will understand you are human. This is another excellent time to model communication skills and how people need to take care of themselves.

Go to your room

This will make your child feel alone and unloved at a time when they need your love and support. Your reason for sending your child away is most likely because of some sort of acting up or bad behavior. Let your child know you recognize they are angry, frustrated, or sad, and then hold them tight. If this doesn't work, tell your child you are going to give them a little time in their room to let out their frustrations. Check in a few minutes later and give more hugs.

72

What were you thinking?

Or "Why would you do that?" or "What's the matter with you?" serve only to belittle your child
and make her feel terrible about herself. Chances
are she was not really thinking at all. When your
children make mistakes or do things they should
not have done, instead of accusing or yelling,
ask them what they might have done differently.
Give them time to reflect; they may not figure
things out right away. Asking this question gives
them an opportunity to problem solve and to revisit a poor choice without making them feel any
worse than they already do.

Wow, that is great!

When your child shows you their latest masterpiece, responding with, "That's beautiful" or, "I love it!" is certainly positive, but it does not convey your engagement. In fact, in some cases, it can even make you seem uninterested or dismissive, surely the opposite of what you hope to communicate. Be specific with your compliments and point out details in your child's work—from art projects to term papers—which will help build their self-esteem.

You are a bad child

Avoid labeling. Telling your daughter she is "bad" because she hit her brother is a message that may stay with her long after the incident has passed. It may even unintentionally become part of how she sees herself—which is probably not what you want! If you must label, keep it to the behavior, not the person. Say "Hitting is bad" rather than "You are bad."

Why didn't you . . . ?

No matter how you fill in the blanks, this question will sound judgmental and will put your children on the defensive. Instead, try helping them come up with a better way to remember a responsibility or whatever was forgotten. Again, this helps children learn to problem solve now and throughout their lives.

76

Lose the word "stupid"

This is one instance where, even if you are talking about a behavior, your children are going to hear and think they are stupid. Any way you use it, it's insulting. If your daughter did do something really stupid, chances are she already knows it. Choose your words carefully; use your best judgment to decide how you will not sound judgmental.

77

Go ask your (other) parent

Without the proper context, sending your child to a different parent can come across as a lack of interest or as dismissive. If your son is asking for permission, tell him you're not sure yet and you'll discuss it with Dad. This allows you and your partner to be on the same page without your child feeling pawned off on the other parent.

It's not what you do for your children,
but what you have taught them to do for themselves
that will make them successful human beings.

—*Ann Landers*

CHAPTER 8

LIFE SKILLS

Dear Sally,

Thank you for giving me the beautiful red sweater for my birthday. I love it and i'm going to wear it to school on Monday.

Please come see us again soon.

Love, Amy

78

Write thank you notes

Someday, when the US Post Office becomes obsolete, snail mail thank you notes can be dispensed with, but even then, something equally as thoughtful and personal should take their place. Let children know that handwritten notes are treasures. When anyone bestows a kindness—a gift or even just a great time—putting some extra effort into conveying appreciation is a simple way to make someone feel good.

Teach your kids to use an alarm clock

It is not your job to wake your children. It is merely your job to provide them with the tools they can use to wake up on their own. Start young and let your son know he is a big boy, and you bet he can use an alarm clock. This is a very easy way to give children some power and control over their lives. Older kids can use the alarm feature on their phones. And, very young children can be taught they cannot wake you up until the alarm goes off—an extra treat for you!

Teach your kids to hydrate

Got a headache? Drink water. Feeling tired? Drink water. Hungry even though you just ate? Drink some more water. A glass of water first thing in the morning is a great habit to instill in kids. Don't wait until thirst sets in. Few of us drink enough water, and when we are not sufficiently hydrated, nothing in our body works as well as it could or should. This old saying holds true: your wee should be clear, not yellow!

Be on time

If you can learn to be on time, your kids will learn to be on time as well. If you are rushing around at the last minute, yelling for your kids to pack up and get in the car, this will be their normal. Set the example, and then make sure your kids are on time for school, practice, lessons, doctor appointments, everything. Prepare in advance, build in extra travel time, and keep away from your phone. When you stop to check your email one more time, before you know it, you are late. Set a good example.

82

Remember the importance of sleep

Not only do you need to be well rested, but your children need plenty of sleep as well. Lack of sleep makes for cranky, irritable children. In addition, they will be less engaged, less focused at school, and less able to handle little stressors. Good sleep habits are touted as a cornerstone in the lives of many successful people, so get your kids started on this early.

83

Model patience

Children are not born patient. They learn to be patient, and they learn it from watching you. So, when you are in a slow line at the store or in stand-still traffic on the way to the water park, take a deep breath before you start your rant. Show your child that it is okay to be frustrated by something and still have a sense of humor about it. This will make everyone's life better.

84

Teach your kids how to do their own laundry

Separating lights and darks, measuring the soap, and using the buttons and dials on the washing machine and dryer are all easy ways a young child can pitch in with this neverending chore. Slightly older children can match socks. By middle school, your child should be able to do their own laundry from amassing, to folding, to putting it away. Does that mean they must do their laundry? That's up to you.

85

Skills instead of solutions

Have you ever solved a problem, big or small, and walked away feeling proud? That's the same feeling a child gets every time they conquer something in their world. It makes them more competent, capable, and confident. Every time you solve a problem for your child, you rob them of one of those experiences. Break down and coach the skills needed to solve a problem. If something seems irreparable, ask, "What do you think you (or we) should do next time?" Ask, don't tell. This is mentoring, not fixing.

86

Teach kids to advocate for themselves

Coach your child in the skills required to get what they need in the world. This can start with having them ask to borrow another child's shovel at the beach and evolve into encouraging them to talk to teachers, coaches, store clerks, and other parents. Role play early on, so they feel comfortable. When children can advocate for themselves, they can create situations in which they can thrive. Each time they do, they become better and more comfortable at it.

87

Teach OHIO—Only Handle It Once

A dirty plate skips the sink and goes right in the dishwasher. A coat comes off, skips the living room chair, and goes straight to a hook or hanger. Open a box, put the contents away, and toss the box in the garbage. Having a fun way to remind your child (and everyone in the house) of a rule or life skill makes it sound less like nagging and more like a secret code. Putting things away begins with knowing where things go. Remember, a place for everything and everything in its place. And, sometimes that place is in the trash.

Foster independent travelers

Just as you taught them to order food for themselves and do their own laundry, you can help
your children become competent, savvy travel-
ers. Sit with your young children and make a list
of what they want to bring on family trips. As
they get older, let them pack for themselves. If
you're adventurous, you can even assign parts
of your vacation itinerary to your kids. When
they're in college and need to book a train ticket
home, they will have the confidence to do so.

Teach money skills

Your child needs to learn how to manage money. Allowance is not payment for services, such as doing chores, but rather, it's money you allow your child to have, simply for being a family member. If your daughter has a weekly income, you can teach her how to save for something she wants. She will learn how to valuate toys, candy, make-up, or arcade games. You can guide at first, but try not to judge how the allowance is spent. Let her make mistakes and learn lessons here and now, rather than years from now in real life with credit cards.

Not all feelings are good, and that is okay

Sometimes our children are not happy and, as parents, we often feel the urge to "fix" that. While our instincts drive us to step in, it's important for kids to develop coping skills. It is tough when your child is excluded from a party, does not get a part in the play, or is benched during a game. Be there to acknowledge their feelings and give them a hug, but stay away from interfering phone calls or emails. Once we see our kids can handle unhappy on their own, our anxiety will dissipate, and we won't feel the need to make everything better.

91

Teach a proper greeting

First impressions matter, and making a good one is often simply a matter of knowing how to respond when you're introduced. A warm greeting is simple: Look the person in the eye, smile, and say, "Nice to meet you." The most intimidating part of this is usually maintaining eye contact, which is something you can practice at home. Whether your kids are visiting a new doctor or meeting the parents of a new friend, this is a skill that will give them confidence and serve them for the rest of their lives.

92

Teach good table manners

Good table manners can start with an Internet video on how to use a fork and knife properly. Then, there are a few simple rules you can teach your child, so they will always feel comfortable at any table:

- Put your napkin on your lap

- Wait to eat until everyone is served

- Compliment the cook

- Ask to be excused

- Help clear the table

Bonus points: never sit until the cook is seated.

93

Coach "please" and "thank you"

This may seem obvious, but unfortunately it's not. "Please" and "thank you" can never be said too much. Mastering this simple social skill will put your kids in good stead for their entire lives. Coach them until it is deeply ingrained. Set a good example by thanking parents after a play-date; thank the person who makes dinner; thank the waitress at the diner; thank the bus driver. Please, keep reminding your kids, and thank them as well.

Each day of our lives we make deposits
in the memory banks of our children.

—*Charles R. Swindoll*

CHAPTER 9

FAMILY MANAGEMENT

94

Have a grab-and-go option for breakfast

As your kids get older, they will be less likely to want to sit down for breakfast before school. Having something nutritious around that they can take to eat on the bus or as a snack in school may be more realistic, and it will help keep the peace first thing in the morning. Protein bars, yogurt, fruit and cheese, and trail mix are some ideas. Put these items on your grocery list and pre-make something like pumpkin muffins or hard-boiled eggs over the weekend, so they are ready to go first thing Monday morning.

95

Pack up the night before

Pack whatever you need the night before—and have your children do the same. Homework, musical instrument, sports attire and equipment, snacks, whatever they need to succeed the next day. Think how much more relaxed mornings will be if the backpacks and all the extras are by the door and ready to go. No more scrambling for that missing cleat or the music for after-school band practice. Even if your kids come home before after-school activities, have them pack everything up the night before. Bonus—you will avoid being late!

96

Create routines

Just as we love traditions, most of us love routines, and kids thrive on them. Critical times tend to be in the morning before school and at bedtime. Allowing your kids to be part of establishing the routines will make them more likely to be willing participants. Do they want to make their bed or get dressed first? Put on pajamas or brush their teeth first? Make a chart together (adding pictures for your little ones) and hang it up. Then, stick to it.

97

Create a dressing system

Fighting with your kids about what they should wear is no fun at all. Try giving your children some control over their attire by creating three different categories:

- Wear anything

- Nice Casual

- Dressy

Once your child knows which clothes fit into each category, let them select for themselves. You'll avoid arguments and be teaching them it is important to dress appropriately for different occasions.

98

Make dinner plans

Take some stress out of mealtimes by minimizing how often you need to ask yourself what you're going to make for dinner. Keep a list of successful meals and rotate through them. You can also relegate a certain dish or type of dish to a day of the week, such as Meatless Mondays or Taco Tuesdays. Maybe there is one day each week where you serve something completely new like New Food Fridays. Let the kids be involved in this plan as well.

99

Archive electronically

Store your child's creations electronically. You can include every piece of art, like every gold-starred homework sheet, or only the ones you both love, like the Mother's Day poems you were given. Apps are available for just this purpose, probably developed by parents who either suffered extreme guilt about throwing away anything sentimental or did not have enough closet space for the myriad plastic bins needed to contain a lifetime of Cheerio art.

100

Create a notebook to organize milestone materials

Make each of your children a loose-leaf notebook with file folders for each grade. Include their annual doctor's report, school and team photos, report cards and any special certificates. When your child is done with high school, you will have documentation of all the important records. And, when they move into their own place, it makes a fun gift to pass on.

Childhood is a short season.

—*Helen Hayes*

One Last Tip

101

Love 'em every chance you get

Before you know it, they will be grown and start-ing their own lives. Grab that hug at every op-portunity. In fact, try not to leave the house with-out a hug, a kiss, or an "I love you." It's unlikely you will ever regret making this effort, no matter how pressed you are for time. You will always be your child's parent, but your time together really does go fast.

Acknowledgments

I am lucky to have been able to continue to learn and grow as a parent from my own mistakes as well as from the mistakes and examples of my dear friends (you know who you are)! I am grateful to my husband, Bill, for his always valuable perspective and endless support. My own children, Victoria and Hudson, are now young adults, and I appreciate having such good-natured test subjects who always showed me the error of my ways. They have taught me that good parenting is a constant, lifelong, learning process and that the true sign of "success" is not that your children are "perfect," but rather that they are happy, capable, and kind.

Thank you to Dayna Steele for giving me the original idea for writing this book and encouraging me to make it happen. Thanks to Jessica Wolf, who went through every tip and rewrote them to have a consistent voice and a touch of humor. Thank you to Angela Engel, Elisabeth Saake, Amy Treadwell, and the rest of the Collective Book Studio team for helping me create such a beautiful book.